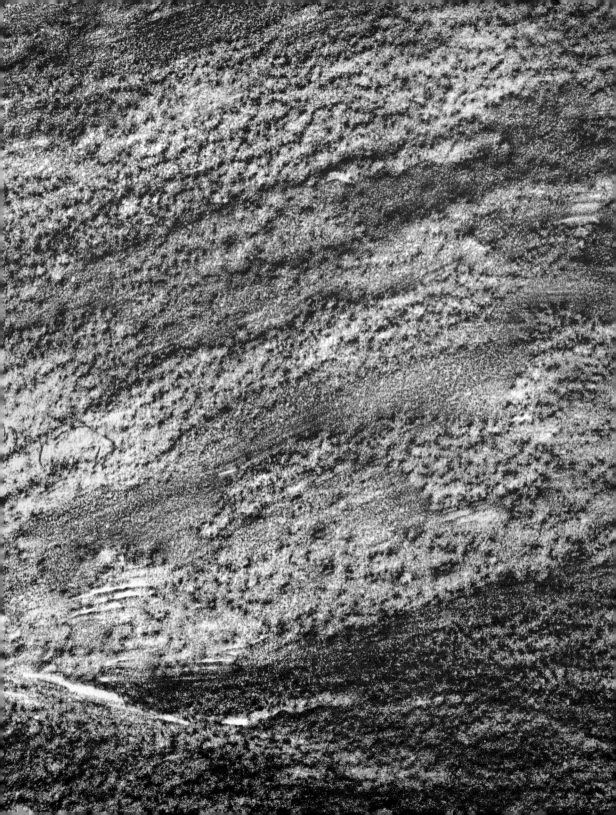

Other books by Alice Dickinson

THE FIRST BOOK OF PREHISTORIC ANIMALS

THE FIRST BOOK OF PLANTS

The FIRST BOOK of
STONE AGE MAN

Late Paleolithic man was an artist.

The FIRST BOOK of
STONE AGE MAN

by ALICE DICKINSON

Pictures by Lorence Bjorklund

FRANKLIN WATTS, INC.
575 Lexington Avenue • New York 22

Library of Congress Catalog Card Number: 62-10062
© Copyright 1962 by Franklin Watts, Inc.
Printed in the United States of America
by the Polygraphic Company of America

4   5   6   7

Contents

In the Beginning

WE HUMAN BEINGS take ourselves very much for granted.

"Of course," we think, "we're in control here. We've cleared the forests and planted the prairies and built dams and roads, and changed the face of the earth to suit ourselves. We've conquered the animals. We can make light in the darkness, and fly through the skies faster than the birds. We can read and write and build enormous skyscrapers and send voices and music hundreds of miles through the air. We own the earth!"

We often forget that the earth is very, very old — probably close to five billion years old — and that for most of that time there were no human beings on it. Human beings are very late comers to the old, old earth. When they began their life on this planet they knew little more than the beasts of the forest. They had everything to learn, and they learned it slowly, and often painfully.

For many millions of years after the beginning of our planet there was no life of any kind on it. At last, however, somehow, somewhere in the water, life started. No one is quite sure how this happened, or what the first life on earth was like. As time went on, though, many different kinds of plants and animals developed, first in the water, and later on land. The earliest fishes probably first appeared from 400 to 500 million years ago; the earliest reptiles, close to 300 million years ago; the earliest of the animals we call mammals, 150 million years ago.

But the earliest men are *less than two* million years old.

Very little is known about these earliest men. Since they could neither read nor write, they left no recorded history of themselves. They lived in what are called *prehistoric times* — that is, the times "before history."

But although we can never know their full story, what we do know is just as surely a part of our own history as are all the recorded happenings of later times. The early human beings started man on the long road of learning and thinking and doing that has brought him to where he is today.

What, then, do we know about these early men? And how do we know it?

All we have as clues to the life of the earliest men are some of their mineralized bones and teeth, the bones of animals that lived at the same time — some of which they ate — some rocks which they left shaped in very special ways, and a few nuts and the seeds of berries which they used as food. No other remains have lasted through the ages.

The few remains that we have are scanty clues to what the earliest men were like, and they mean little to ordinary people. There are scientists who are trained to read meaning from them, however. Some of the scientists have studied the beginnings and development of mankind. From the early bones and teeth — their shape and size, the way in which the bones were joined together, and the manner in which the muscles seem to have been attached to them — they can tell some things about early man. These scientists who

Archeologists look for traces of early man.

are experts in the development and races of man are called *anthropologists*.

Another group of scientists studies everything that man has left behind him: the places where he lived, the objects that he made, and any other traces, however small. These scientists are trained to look for a meaning in even the tiniest clue. And, from all the clues that they find assembled in one place, they try to piece together the way of life of the men who lived there. These scientists are called *archeologists*.

Besides human bones, there have been found in various places the bones of other creatures which are like men in some ways. These creatures might be called "man-like." Some of their bones are much older than those of the earliest men.

Judging by what scientists have learned from all the bones — man and man-like — it seems clear that human beings have developed from some more ancient animal. As yet, no one is exactly sure what that animal was. Scientists believe it was a member of the tree-climbing primate family, who took to the ground. Over millions of years, its descendants slowly changed until finally they developed into man.

Changing of this sort has happened often in the long story of animals on earth. This is how it comes about. Among animals of a single kind there is occasionally one who is born with something unusual in the way its body is formed — something that makes it slightly different from its parents. Very likely the slight difference is a harmful one, which causes the animal's death.

But, on the other hand, sometimes the little difference, called a *mutation,* is a favorable one which helps its possessor to do even better in its surroundings than its parents did. When this animal has children, they may be born with the same body difference. They will also do well.

As time goes on, their children and grandchildren and great-grandchildren may not only inherit their parents' differences, but may also occasionally be born with some new body change. Perhaps, in the meantime, the climate has shifted a bit, and this body change is an advantage in living under the new weather conditions. In that case, the animals will flourish. Their children will probably inherit the same characteristic and pass it along to their children.

Thus, slowly, over millions of years, all the little differences that have been inherited from one generation to another will add up to so large a change that the result will be a new species of animal, quite unlike its ancient ancestor who started with one slight difference.

The primate animal that developed into man may have changed very gradually in this way. We do not know just what took place.

We do know this, however: at some point less than two million years ago, man did finally come into being — a creature unlike any other animal, with wonderful differences that have helped him become what he is today.

What Makes Man?

WHAT ARE man's differences?

First: *Man can stand upright and walk on two legs.* No other animal can walk this way all the time, though some animals do it occasionally. In order to do it, man must have a remarkable sense of balance. The shape of his spine, of his foot, and of other parts of his skeleton makes this balance possible.

Second: *Man has grasping hands.* Because he walks on his hind legs, his front legs — or arms — have been freed to do other things. Each arm can reach in almost any direction. And, at the end of each arm, a hand with four fingers and a thumb can stretch wide or close into a fist. The thumb is at right angles to the fingers. When it is moved to press against them, the hand is able to grasp and hold things.

Third: *Man has what is called "stereoscopic vision."* Many animals have their eyes at the sides of their heads, each looking in a

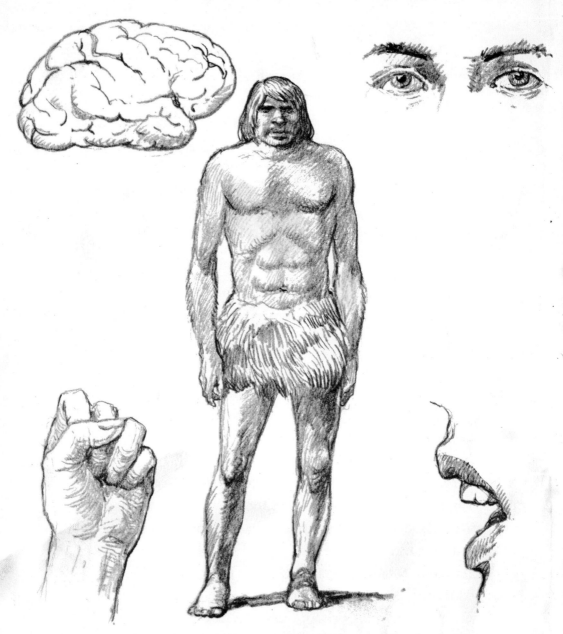

Man can stand upright and walk on two legs. He has grasping hands, stereoscopic vision, a highly developed brain, and he communicates with words. It is not known when man first started to use language.

different direction. They see two images — one with each eye. But man's eyes are placed side by side, both looking in the same direction. The pictures he sees, one with each eye, overlap and form one image of whatever he is focusing on. This kind of vision, called *stereoscopic*, is helpful in judging distances and depths. Without his stereoscopic eyes, which can also see colors, man's grasping hands would be of much less use in holding an object and working with it.

Fourth: *Man has a highly developed brain*. Because of this, he is a very good learner. He can store in his brain all the knowledge brought him through his stereoscopic eyes, his feeling, grasping hands, and in other ways. By reasoning about his knowledge, he can fit pieces of it together into new patterns — to develop new ideas and to invent new objects and new ways of doing things. He can remember, and think, and plan ahead for things that may happen in the future.

Fifth: *Man can talk*. He has language. It is true that other animals have sounds for communicating with one another. But each kind of animal has only a few different sounds — one for each of a small number of happenings. There may be, among others, a sound to warn off enemies; a sound to summon friends; a mating call. The sounds do not change from one generation to another, and no new ones are added.

Man's language is different. He can make many sounds. And he has a brain that can invent as many names, or words, as he needs for his actions and objects and ideas. He can add new words to his language whenever he wishes.

No one knows when man first began to talk. The early men may not have had language. It is probable, however, that without gradually learning to talk, man could not have advanced to the position he holds today. With words, men tell one another their experiences and ideas. With words they build up their knowledge, and with words they pass it on to their children. With words they do their thinking.

Here, then, is man, balancing upright on two strong legs. With his grasping hands he holds objects and feels their shape and size and material. With his stereoscopic eyes he sees the world around him and is able to judge spaces and distances and depths. His well-developed brain directs his activities and receives the information he gathers. And his brain remembers the information, puts it into

Man, with his superior eyes and brain, his grasping hands, and his upright position, has been able to make and use tools.

words, and from it forms ideas, which he passes on to other people, chiefly through language.

Man's hands, his superior eyes, his brain, and his upright position made it possible for him to do something no other animal could. Man learned to make and use tools — crude clubs and roughly chipped stones, at first. These tools took the place of the animals' fangs and claws and teeth, and they served man much better. If conditions around him changed as time went on, man could change his tools, too, and invent more suitable ones — something the animals could not do.

By making and using tools, early man was able to protect himself from the beasts of prey, to hunt his food, and to survive and slowly advance. And, over the thousands of years, he was able to find new ways of making use of the natural world around him. Man's ability as a toolmaker is one of the important things that has set him apart from the animals.

The Earliest Men Yet Known

THERE SEEM to have been various types of very early men — all unlike men as they look today. The bones of the earliest ones yet known were found in East Africa in 1959 and 1960, by Dr. Louis S. B. Leakey and his wife and son.

For years the Leakeys had been combing the slopes of Olduvai Gorge, in Tanganyika, uncovering ancient stone tools and the bones of extinct animals — but always searching for one thing: some part of the men who had made the tools. At last, one thrilling day —

250 feet down in the gorge — Mrs. Leakey spied two enormous human teeth gleaming in the face of the rock.

She and Dr. Leakey immediately looked further. In addition to a foot-long piece of a man's shinbone, they found a nearly complete human skull embedded in the rock, among ancient stone tools and animal bones. The rock had pressed on the skull and broken it into over four hundred pieces, however, and for weeks the searchers sifted tons of rubble in order not to lose any of the precious fragments.

Putting the pieces of bone together again was like working on an especially fascinating jigsaw puzzle. Gradually the Leakeys watched the skull of a low-browed, long-faced young man take shape. They named him *Zinjanthropus*. (*Zinj* is Arabic for "East Africa"; *anthropus* means "man.")

Head and face of Zinjanthropus, *reconstructed from the skull* (*left*). (After Leakey)

Because his skull is fully developed, yet his wisdom teeth show no wear, scientists believe that *Zinjanthropus* was about eighteen years old. He was evidently about five feet tall and walked fully upright. Although he had almost no forehead, his skull was roomy enough for a fair-sized brain. It is not known whether he could talk.

The remains of *Zinjanthropus* were found at a campsite on the shores of an ancient lake. Soon after he died, his body had evidently been covered by rising water and mud, which preserved his bones and prevented them from being carried away by wild animals. Over the thousands of years they became buried deeper in the earth, until finally Olduvai Gorge formed, and at least some of the bones were uncovered.

Zinjanthropus lived out of doors and, as the climate was warm, he probably wore no clothes. Wild berries and nuts were evidently his chief food, but he was beginning to try meat eating. He killed small, easily captured animals such as lizards and mice, which he may have skinned with his roughly chipped stone tools before eating them raw.

His life was very simple. Yet he was thinking of the world in which he lived and, with his tools, was trying to master it. And he was experimenting with food — finding out which plants were safe to eat and which were deadly and should be left alone, and what animals might be used. He was taking the first faltering steps toward gaining control of his surroundings.

In 1960, while uncovering the ancient bones of a saber-toothed tiger, Dr. Leakey, his wife, and his nineteen-year-old son made still

Zinjanthropus *lived in open campsites.*

another find at Olduvai Gorge. In a layer of rock even older than that in which the bones of *Zinjanthropus* were embedded they discovered the remains of a grown-up and a child — probably about eleven years old — with tools.

Tests made on the rock in which the remains were found show that these earliest humans we yet know were probably over one million years old.

From South Africa come the remains of another whole group of very early, very primitive creatures called the *australopithecines*. The various types differ one from another, but all of them seem to have stood upright, and their brains were at least a little larger than those of their animal ancestors. One of these types, *Australopithecus prometheus*, is thought to have lived about 600,000 years ago. He seems to have used very crude tools and to have eaten birds' eggs and the raw meat of whatever animals he could kill.

Peking Man

THE BONES of other early men have been found in Java, and in China, near Peking. These two types of men were much alike. More is known about Peking man than Java man because scientists exploring a quarry near Peking were fortunate enough to discover a cave dwelling from 200,000 to 300,000 years old.

Parts of over forty skeletons were found there, and from them anthropologists have gained a good idea of Peking man's appearance. They say he was about five feet four inches tall, and walked on slightly bowed legs. He had a thick, rather flat skull; a very low, sloping forehead; a jutting, bony ridge over his eyes; a heavy jaw, large teeth, and almost no chin. His brain case was rather small; yet anthropologists say, judging from its appearance, he could possibly talk at least a little.

Peking man was a great meat eater and a mighty hunter, though no one knows how he killed his prey. The floor of his cave was thickly strewn with the bones of large animals, mostly deer. But there were also the remains of bison, horse, wild boar, leopard, tiger, hyena, bear, rhinoceros, elephant, and camel. Many of the bones had been split so that the cave dwellers could eat the marrow inside them.

Peking man was neither tidy nor fastidious. As he finished eating, he evidently tossed the bones aside, to lie where they fell on the floor of his cave. He lived in a mess, and it must have smelled awful. Scattered in with the animal bones, moreover, were those of Peking man himself — and they were split for marrow, too. From the evidence, it appears that Peking man was a cannibal.

He lived an animal's life, you are probably thinking.

Yet he made tools, and he knew the use of fire.

Most of the thousands of tools scattered on the cave floor were made from lumps of quartz, green sandstone, and limestone, collected from the countryside round about. To shape them, Peking man placed each one on an anvil stone and with a hammer stone broke it to a proper size for grasping. He struck a few end chips from many of the stones. The result was a crude "chopper," with one end slightly sharpened to make a rough cutting edge. Choppers

Peking man was a great meat eater and a mighty hunter.

A chopper.

were probably used for many purposes: digging, scraping, hacking, cutting — whatever was necessary.

Besides the choppers, Peking man had a few very crude flakes of stone which he probably used for scraping and cutting. He also broke pieces of bone raggedly so that they might serve as tools. Possibly he used pieces of wood for clubs and spears, but wood is too perishable to have lasted. In any case, his tools were rough. They do show, however, that he had a plan in mind when he made them, and that he was able to carry it out, though not very skillfully.

Among the stones and bones on the cave floor were black streaks of charcoal, showing hearths. Even in that distant time, man had learned to tame fire, a wild force that terrified the animals and could destroy a forest.

No one knows whether Peking man could ignite a fire whenever he wanted. More probably, he captured a flame already burning, perhaps as the result of a lightning flash or the rubbing together of two dry tree branches. From then on, he had only to preserve it and keep it from dying.

In any case, he had experimented with nature, and had taken a huge step forward. He had found out how to get fire and how to keep it going: what substances to burn, how often to feed it, how to prevent it from spreading too far.

And he was getting some idea of fire's many uses. It gave warmth. It lighted the dark corners of his cave. It frightened man-eating animals away from his home.

Perhaps he had already discovered that he could harden a wooden spear by holding its point in the fire's heat. Whether he had found that fire would cook his meat is not known.

He was experimenting in other ways, too. Among the litter in his cave were the seeds of hackberries, a fruit he apparently used as food. Like *Zinjanthropus* before him, he had begun to know what plants were safe to eat.

Glacial Europe

AT THE PRESENT TIME, the rest of our scanty knowledge about the very early men comes chiefly from Europe. True, remains have been found in Africa and Asia also, but in Europe there has been a more widespread searching than elsewhere. Only a very few bones of the early people have been found there. Mostly, the discoveries have been tools — thousands upon thousands of stones, chipped by man into shapes useful for doing various chores.

These tools have given the name, *Stone Age*, to that faraway time when they were made. The first part of that period, when man shaped his tools by chipping and flaking, is called the *Paleolithic*, or *Old Stone, Age*. (*Paleo* means "old"; *lithic* means "stone.") In those ancient days, nothing was known about the use of metals. A stone, a stick, or a piece of bone were the things that came easiest to hand when a man wished to kill an animal, grub out a root, or perform some other task. Men may have made tools from wood, too, but only the stone ones have lasted over the many thousands of years.

Experts who have studied the land, the rocks, the mountains, and the valleys of Europe have learned a great deal about the climate during the Stone Age. The story of what happened is recorded forever in scratches on the rocks, in the shape of the hills and valleys, and in the general lay of the land.

Four times during the past one million years the temperature on the earth dropped. Then, for periods possibly as long as two hundred thousand years, the winters became long and bitterly cold and the summers short and very cool. Snowfall increased, and the snow that fell in the polar regions and on high mountains had almost no chance to melt. Over the years it piled up into great sheets of ice.

Just south of the glaciers, cold-weather animals gathered.

As layers upon layers of the snow and ice accumulated, glaciers — great rivers of ice — were formed. Slowly they flowed out from the polar regions, and down the mountain passes. Four times, the northern part of Europe was covered with an enormous sheet of ice, possibly as much as a mile thick. From the Alps a smaller ice sheet spread completely over what is now Switzerland, and covered parts of France, Germany, Austria, and Italy. Just south of the glaciers, cold winds blew and cold-weather animals gathered. Living was hard.

But between the four long cold periods, there were warmer times. Then, starting at their southernmost edges, the glaciers gradually melted. Europe became free of ice once more, and the warm-weather plants and animals returned.

All of this changing from cold to warm to cold, and back again, took place very, very slowly until, about ten thousand years ago, the latest of the glaciers had finished melting back and once more Europe entered a warmer spell, which has continued into our time.

Of very early man in Europe, dating from perhaps 400,000 years ago, nothing much is known excepting his tools, although there is one other clue — a lower jawbone with its teeth still in place, discovered 79 feet down in a sandpit near Heidelberg, Germany. With so little to go on, it is difficult to tell much about the creature who left this bone. The jaw is heavy and chinless, and the teeth are those of a human.

Heidelberg jaw.

The oldest of the tools are found along the rivers, on open terraces where the prehistoric early Europeans evidently camped out. Apparently dating from the same time are the bones of elephants, lions, and other animals of warm regions. The climate must have been mild then, between the melting back of one glacier and the onset of another.

The early people probably lived in a "catch-as-catch-can" way, wandering about in small bands, searching for food. They must have been hunters and "gatherers," killing animals — small ones, at first — and gathering anything that could be eaten: berries, seeds, nuts, roots, fruit, birds' eggs, snails, perhaps even grubs and insects. Living by hunting is usually chancy, and there are times when any food that will keep a person alive is welcome. Like *Zinjanthropus* and Peking man, these people came to know what was safe to eat and where it could be found. And they slowly gained skill in hunting game.

Probably by experimenting, they seem to have discovered that flint was the best stone for making tools. It is fine-grained and very hard, and can quite easily be chipped.

The common early tools in Europe were big, crude objects, now called *hand axes*. At one end they had a heavy butt for grasping with the fingers; at the other end they were chipped on both sides to make a rounded or pointed tip. Hand axes did not really serve as axes. They were probably an all-purpose tool, equally good for digging up a root, cracking a nut, or cutting up a dead animal.

As the thousands of years went by, the workmanship on the hand axes became better. They grew smaller and were trimmed to an

Hand ax.

oval or almond shape, with a sharp, thin edge.

In addition to the hand axes, *flake tools* began gradually to appear. They were made by striking pieces from a larger stone. Once the worker got the knack, he could produce broad, thin flakes of flint with a good cutting edge, which he could touch up by a little chipping, if he wished. Flake tools were good for scraping and chopping and cutting.

Every man must have been his own toolmaker, shaping new flints as often as his old ones were lost or dulled or nicked — perhaps as often as every day. As time went on, flakes seem to have won out over hand axes as the popular tool. But thousands of years went by with very little change in man's ways of doing things — or so it appears from all the evidence.

Flake tools.

The Neanderthal People

DATING from somewhere between 200,000 and 150,000 years ago are parts of a young woman's skull, found at Swanscombe, England. Though the skull bones are very thick, they seem to be surprisingly like those of modern humans in some ways. A skull found in Steinheim, Germany, is about the same age, but not as modern in appearance. And at Fontéchevade, in France, two skulls have been found, of a little later date. One of these looks quite modern. Not a great deal can be told about how any of these people lived.

Beginning about 100,000 years ago, however, there are many more clues to the people who were to be found in Europe at that time. Anthropologists call them the *Neanderthal* (Nee-AN-der-tal) people, or *Neanderthalers,* because the first recognized trace of them was a piece of skull dug out of a gravel pit in the Neander River valley in Germany. (In German, *thal* means "valley": hence, Neanderthal.)

Swanscombe skull (left); and a Neanderthal skull (right).

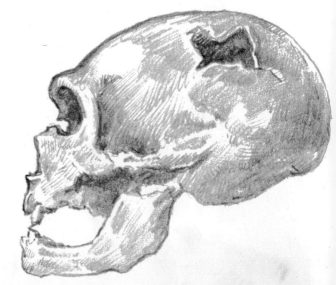

Since that find — the year was 1856 — archeologists have unearthed the remains of about one hundred persons who might be called Neanderthal. They have been found scattered throughout Europe, in Asia, and in North Africa.

Probably the earliest of the Neanderthalers lived when the climate was warm, between the third and fourth glaciations. But when the ice sheet once more began inching and grinding down over Europe, these people did not flee to the south. Instead, they took to caves and learned to fight the cold. It is our good fortune that they did, as caves are fine places for preserving ancient bones which in more open spots might have been scattered and lost.

Inasmuch as the remains of the Neanderthalers range everywhere from a single tooth to complete skeletons, the anthropologists have been able to take a good look at these people. They find that the European Neanderthalers were heavy and stocky, with barrel chests. Their skulls were peculiar — long and low and wide. For all their shape, however, these skulls provided room for a good-sized brain.

As to faces, those of the European Neanderthalers were long and rather flat, with broad noses, oversized jaws, jutting brows, and not much chin or forehead.

Not all the Neanderthalers were alike, however. Those of Asia seem to have been taller and less heavy. They had more forehead and chin, and their skulls were shaped a little more like those of modern men.

Like the earlier men, the Neanderthal people had both hand axes and flakes. Some of the flake tools were points, in the rough shape of triangles, and some were sidescrapers with one curved edge, espe-

Neanderthal head and face, reconstructed from the skull (right).

cially good for scraping various materials. Both were fashioned with a good deal of skill.

The points probably served as knives for skinning and cutting up animals killed by the hunters. Among other things, the scrapers may possibly have been used in preparing the skins of animals for wearing as wraps. In the frigid Europe of glacier days, the Neanderthal people may have started covering their bodies with the fur of the creatures they killed.

Aside from stone tools, it seems probable that the hunters had pointed wooden spears. Some archeologists think that they may have attached their stone points to long wooden handles and thus made flint-tipped spears. Others do not see how the points could have been fastened securely enough to be of any use.

Whatever they used as weapons, the Neanderthal people seem to have been excellent hunters, killing large animals such as mammoths and woolly rhinoceroses. It may be that they caught these beasts in pitfall traps, or cornered them in canyons, and slaughtered them before they could escape.

A mammoth was a good-sized animal of the elephant family, about the size of a circus elephant today. A woolly rhinoceros was also large. Either of them would have been hard to kill with the weapons the Neanderthal men had. Such a fierce creature, wounded and angry and thrashing around, could easily trample any hunter who might get in its way. And certainly no one person would tackle such prey singlehanded. Neanderthal men must have made their brains help their brawn: they probably organized their hunts carefully, and had a plan of action, obeying one man who acted as leader. They must have been able to work together as a band.

Once the animal was killed, they seem to have cut it up and brought only certain parts into the caves. The meat served as food. They saved some of the larger bones for anvils and chopping blocks, and broke others roughly for use as tools. But they did no real fashioning of bone into helpful shapes.

The many hearths in the Neanderthal caves show that these people commonly used fire to keep themselves warm and to frighten away any animals who may also have sought undercover protection

Neanderthal tools.

The Neanderthal men probably hunted in bands.

from the cold. Possibly they also cooked their food, although many archeologists doubt this.

What did these Neanderthal people think about? How much could they talk? These are things we shall never know entirely.

They buried their dead and sometimes put objects in the graves. They evidently thought about death and were concerned about what happened to the dead.

Though we know little about the Neanderthalers, of one thing we can be sure. They were thoughtfully facing life's problems and trying to solve them. Their hunting, their toolmaking, their living in caves, their use of fire, their care of the dead — all these activities show what steps they had taken.

Enter Homo Sapiens

THE NEANDERTHAL people were only partly successful, however. There came a time during the fourth glaciation when for a while the climate was warmer. During this period the Neanderthalers mysteriously disappeared from the face of the earth. After a certain point in time, there is no longer any sign of them.

Everywhere, starting between 50,000 and 30,000 years ago, the remains that are found are no longer those of Neanderthalers, but of an entirely different species of men. They are men who are modern in appearance, and they seem already to be divided into several racial groups. They have our posture and our head shapes — complete with real foreheads, well-formed chins, skulls with roomy brain cases, and almost no bony brow ridges. They are "our kind of men," and anthropologists call them by the same scientific name we have: *Homo sapiens,* Latin for "wise man."

Anthropologists have differing ideas about where *Homo sapiens* came from, and why he suddenly appeared in Europe at the time of the fourth glaciation. Actually, no one can be certain at this point. More searching and the finding of more skeletons in Africa and elsewhere may clear up the mystery.

We do know this, however: at the beginning of the glacial period there seem to have been several different species of men on earth. At the end of the glacial period, one species alone remained, supreme over all the others: *Homo sapiens.* He has dominated the world ever since.

Early Homo sapiens.

Changing Ways

THE FOURTH, and last, glaciation was a time of changing climate — slow change, to be sure, as the weather gradually grew warmer and the ice sheet drew back . . . only to pile up more snow and advance again as the temperature dropped and cold winds howled from the north.

As the climate changed, the appearance of the land changed, too. When the temperature grew warmer and the glaciers shrank northward, forests grew. When the glaciers returned, the forests died out, and just south of the ice sheet were open "tundras," flat plains covered with low bushes, grasses, and mosses. And, of course, when the temperature and plant life changed, so did the animals, according to which creatures could survive in the particular surroundings of the time. Sometimes there were forest animals who liked mild temperatures. Then again, there were cold-weather animals of the tundra.

At this time there seems to have been a belt of territory inhabited by humans, extending from Spain to North China and bounded on the north by the ever-shifting ice sheet. Within this territory, beginning about 35,000 B.C., groups of people wandered constantly. They appear to have come from Asia — again, we are not sure — and they seem to have spread outward in waves through Europe and North Africa toward the Atlantic Ocean. As group followed different group, each lived according to its own habits. To describe all of these people would be a most complicated business. They did have some things in common, however.

They seem to have been more alert, more at home in their world, and able to get more out of it than any of the people who had gone before them. Partly this may only appear to be so because they left more remains and, as a result, more is known about them. But that is not the whole story.

They had inherited the thousands of years' worth of knowledge that had been collected, stored up, and passed on to them by earlier men, and they were bright enough to put this knowledge to good use. In addition, they had learned to take full advantage of new materials, and especially of the very plentiful animal materials: bone, ivory, antler, teeth, skins, and sinews.

They made many more kinds of tools than earlier men had. And they worked out plans not only for general-purpose tools, but also for tools designed to do one particular job — such as bone needles with eyes, for use in sewing animal skins together. More and more, they were learning to "make their heads save their heels" — and their hands.

They could now plan well enough so that they were making tools designed especially for making other tools. They fashioned pointed awls, for instance, to use for boring the holes in bone needles and other bone tools.

And they had new processes for making tools. They shaped a needle, for example, by gouging out a piece of bone, then rubbing it down with sandstone and polishing it with emery, and finally making a hole in it with an awl.

For all these people, the starting point in making most of their tools was a thin, narrow flint flake with parallel sides, called a *blade*. Like a knife blade, it was much longer than it was wide.

To begin with, toolmakers had probably fashioned a blade only once in a while — by accident — when they happened to strike a piece of flint in a particular way. But they must have seen how much more useful than other kinds of flakes the blades were. And — probably after long experimenting — they hit on a successful way of manufacturing blades whenever they needed them, by knocking them off a flint *core,* trimmed roughly to the shape of a cylinder.

One of the chief advantages of a blade was that it formed a sort of toolmaker's "blank," which could be worked over into many different shapes.

As a blade came from the core, its two parallel sides had sharp edges. Sometimes the toolmaker could use it just as it was. Or, by chipping small pieces from one of the parallel sides — and so, dulling it — he could make himself a knife.

Or, among other things, he could fashion his blade into a *burin* or *graver.* This tool was a blade with its side edges blunted and with one or more small, slanting flakes knocked off one end, to form a sharp edge like a chisel's, backed up by a shoulder.

Flint blades were struck from a core, roughly cylindrical in shape.

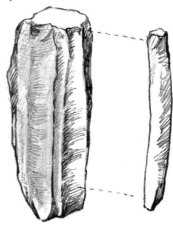

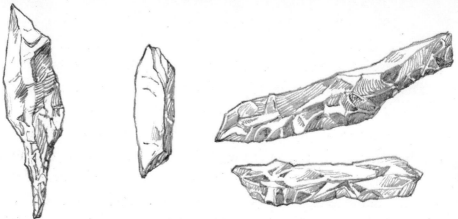

Burins (two at left) and knives, made from blades.

Because the burin's shoulder reinforced the chisel edge and gave it added strength, this tool was especially suited for working with soft wood, and with bone, antler, and ivory.

For some things, bone and antler and ivory were better materials than flint. In hunting, for instance, a flint spearhead often shattered if it hit a hard, unyielding surface. But a bone spearhead was more elastic. If it hit something hard, it had enough "give" so that it would not break. And a bone-tipped spear was lighter to carry than a flint-tipped one.

Bone and antler and ivory often came in large sizes, too, and with them a man could make bigger weapons than he was likely to make with flint.

Besides that, these new materials were easier than flint was to shape in unusual ways, and holes could be bored in them without too much difficulty.

Bone and antler and ivory opened up all kinds of possibilities for new equipment, and men now had good enough tools and lively enough imaginations so that they were ready to experiment with these different materials. Working with a burin, they made a whole new kit of tools and weapons that would have been impossible in flint.

They started out with rather simple things, like polished bone pins and awls, and spear points with the blunt end split so that a shaft could be wedged into it, and the point thus fastened to its handle. Before the Old Stone Age was over, men were making barbed harpoons of antler, fish lures of bone, and other ingenious devices.

Of the people who inhabited the world in this latter part of the Old Stone Age — called the *Upper Paleolithic Age* — most is known about those in the territory that is now Europe. From the remains found in this area, it is plain that, of the varied groups, each lived according to its own customs, and used the tool and weapon kit best suited to its needs and habits. Every once in a while, each probably added whatever new things were made necessary by the changing climate and surroundings.

Bone and ivory tools. From top to bottom: barbed harpoon point; barbed harpoon point; needle; split-based bone point; bone awl.

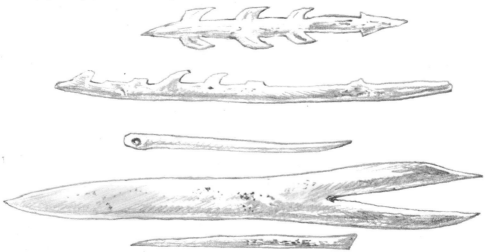

Two groups about whom a fair amount is known are the mammoth hunters of east and central Europe and the Magdalenians of southwestern Europe. A look at them gives an idea of the people of 20,000 years ago and a little later.

The Mammoth Hunters

THE MAMMOTH HUNTERS lived during a glacial period. Near the ice sheet the winters must have been long and harsh and bitterly cold. But there were brief summers, and each summer day was fairly lengthy. The hot sun melted at least the surface and southern edge of the ice, and thousands of rivulets flowed from it. Carried in the little streams were the soil, the ground-up rock, the bits of grass and leaves and bone that had been trapped and frozen into the glacier as it inched forward over the land. Now, freed in the melting water, all this finely ground material rolled southward over the plains. And when autumn came, winds blowing off the ice — before it froze solid again — picked up more of this clutter and whirled it away.

South of the ice sheet, layer after layer of the fine glacial dust settled in a thick, enormously fertile blanket of soil, called loess (LO-ess).

Each spring, as the sun grew warmer, millions of plants poked up through the loess. There was a sudden, almost dazzling burst of greenery and a brief budding and blossoming as the mosses, the grasses, the rushes, the sedges, and the flowering herbs lived out their brief season.

Here were rich pastures for the huge herds of grazing animals that were so plentiful in those days. With the coming of spring, these creatures surged from their sheltered winter grounds farther south, to feed on the lush new growth.

There were throngs of the large plant eaters such as mammoths, bison, wild horses, wild cattle, reindeer, and musk oxen. Besides them, on the plains were small animals such as hares, and flocks of wild fowl such as ducks and geese and arctic grouse. And, attracted by the chance to prey on the plant-eating animals, there were meat eaters such as wolves and foxes.

This was ideal game country for human hunters, too, if they could withstand the climate. For a small group of people, a large creature such as a mammoth or a bison could solve the food problem nicely for several days. Men brave and crafty enough to kill even a single animal were well rewarded.

And there was much that a creature could provide besides meat. Its bones served not only for tool- and weaponmaking, but for other purposes as well. More and more uses were being found for sinews and skins. Reindeer had antlers — excellent material for tools and weapons. Mammoths had ivory tusks sometimes ten feet long. Ivory was a fine-grained material that could be readily carved and that took a high polish; workmen had already discovered its beauty as well as its value for practical purposes.

It was possible for men to get a whole living from these large herds of animals, and that is just what the mammoth hunters did. They had watched the herds closely and knew their habits. North in the summer — south in the winter — slowly the animals ate

The mammoth hunters lay in wait at the passes through which the beasts must go.

their way. And always they followed the same routes through mountain passes and along a level corridor of land between their winter feeding grounds in what is now the Danube River valley and their summer pastures farther north.

In the summer the mammoth hunters followed the herds over the plains, moving as the animals moved. Perhaps they slept in the open, or possibly in tents made of animal skins stretched over supports of mammoth bone.

When the warm days were over, however, a more substantial shelter than a tent was needed. And here the hunters showed their skill at planning.

At the vital passes through which the crowding herds must file twice a year as they migrated north and south, these people set up permanent camps. These were sheltered from the icy northern wind, yet located at the points where the animals might most easily be trapped. The success of the hunters' scheming is seen in the thousands and thousands of animal bones still buried in the loess at these places.

Of the bones, three-quarters are those of mammoths. These people were mammoth specialists, and their whole life depended on the enormous creatures. At one of the campsites, the hunters had sorted and stacked the bones for use: tusks in one pile, hipbones in another, shoulder blades in another, and so on.

At some points in southern Russia and Czechoslovakia the remains of the winter houses can still be seen — perhaps the first houses ever to be built. They were made by digging large circular pits three or four feet deep in the soft loess, and lining them with

The mammoth hunters lived in pit houses, probably roofed over with skins or turf.

mammoth shoulder blades or stone slabs. Placing the floors underground in this way provided the dwellers with good protection from cold winds, and made the shelters easier to build.

The roofs are no longer in place, but they were probably made by draping skins or piling turf over a framework of bones or tusks, and banking the whole structure with earth. Inside the houses the hunters built hearths with flues, thus furnishing drafts to make their fires burn more easily.

Among the bones other than those of mammoths are many of wolves and foxes. These are not good food animals, but they do have excellent fur. And among the tools are many scrapers, and strong bone needles which must have been used for sewing, with animal sinews as thread. These hunting people probably cured animal skins and fashioned them into fur clothing of some kind, although no one today knows what it was like.

No one knows how the hunters caught the giant mammoths, either. The beasts may have been trapped in pitfalls or they may have been stampeded into gullies or over cliffs, then killed with a blow from a rock or a stab from a spear. A great many of the bones are those of young, inexperienced animals — the ones that might most easily be tricked. A group of skilled hunters who had observed their prey keenly would find a way to outwit these creatures, if they all worked together. These men had to cooperate closely.

Following the mammoths must have been a strenuous and sometimes a dangerous way of living, yet it must have been a good way, too. As the seasons rolled by, the mammoths — who furnished food, shelter, fuel, and much else — could be counted on. As surely as warm weather came, they would appear, grazing slowly northward. Then, for the hunters, came the roving summer under the open skies; and in the fall, the return to the snug hunting camps, and the storing of the winter's supply of meat, to be buried safely in the snowdrifts.

Hunters trailing a wounded animal.

Busy as this life kept the people, it did bring them some security. And it did leave them some time to think about themselves, their fellow hunters, and their world.

At one of the campsites, a grave was uncovered in which twenty human skeletons were found, lying on their sides as if they were asleep. The spot was fenced in with mammoth shoulder blades, and covered with a layer of stones to keep out thieving animals. One young man wore a beautifully polished necklace of grooved ivory beads.

In another grave, a single skeleton of a young man was found. He was splendidly decorated with cockleshell beads and many tiny disks of stone and ivory. Just above his body lay the tusk and shoulder blade of a mammoth — the beast that was the source of life for his people. His fellow hunters had given him in death the good things he had enjoyed in life, even to the finery. They had a warm feeling for their comrades. When these friends died, the living expressed their sorrow by arranging a good resting place for them.

In their leisure time the mammoth hunters were craftsmen and artists. They carved themselves ivory bracelets and beads, decorated with patterns of lines and circles; and they made headdresses and necklaces of shells and animals' teeth, pierced with holes and strung together with animal sinews. They were thinking, feeling people, and like all human beings, they considered themselves important — worthy to be decorated with these fine things that they made with their hands.

The Magdalenian Cave Dwellers

THE MAGDALENIANS lived a little later than the mammoth hunters, but still in chilly glacial weather. Archeologists have named them for La Madeleine, a spot in France where many remains of their life have been found.

While it is true that the Magdalenians spread over a wide part of southwestern Europe, they seem to have centered in what are now southwestern France and neighboring parts of Spain. In the grassy valleys of the Dordogne, the Vezère, and other rivers there was perfect country for people who lived by hunting. Salmon ran up the streams each spring. On either side of the pleasant valleys rose limestone cliffs, pitted with caves and rocky hollows, and containing a good supply of flint. And on top of the cliffs were the plains where herds of reindeer, bison, wild horses, mammoths, musk oxen, and other game animals grazed. Both food and shelter were here for the taking, and the Magdalenians made themselves a good life in these valleys, as many earlier groups of people had before them.

The caves in the cliffs offered fine shelter as long as families lived near their entrances. Farther back, it was dark and clammy, and there was no way for campfire smoke to escape. The black depths of the caverns were frightening, too, and threatened all kinds of unseen dangers such as lurking animals.

The places that were open, yet sheltered with a slanting roof of rock — an overhang — were perhaps even better as homes. These spots were especially good if they were on the south side of a valley.

Caves and overhangs in the cliffs made good homes for the Magdalenians.

In winter they were warmed by the rays of the low-lying sun — and in bitter weather a windbreak could always be built. At the same time, a good draft blew the hearth smoke away. In summer, when the sun was higher, the overhang of rock provided shade, and the dwellers could enjoy any breeze that blew. All year round, there was a good view up and down the valley — an advantage to hunters always on the lookout for grazing animals.

In their earlier days, when the ice sheets had moved far south, the Magdalenians mainly hunted reindeer. After a long time, however, the glaciers began slowly to melt northward, and the reindeer followed them. Then the people changed to hunting other animals, chiefly bison and horses. Besides the large animals, they sometimes caught arctic grouse and hares, and they fished the streams for trout and salmon.

These people were great workers in bone, ivory, and antler, and they made many ingenious objects to help them in their hunting. Their chief weapon was a spear with a sharp bone point. As time went on, the hunters made more elaborate points, with barbs, and finally were fashioning harpoon points with saw teeth and prongs.

For casting their spears, the hunters made spear throwers. These were rods of bone or horn, each with a hook at one end, against

A spear thrower.

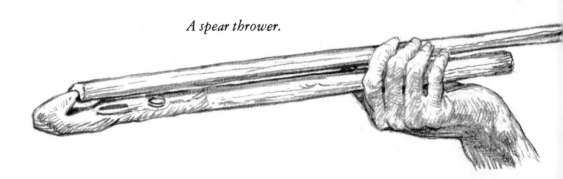

The hunters used spears with bone points.

which the butt of a spear shaft would fit. A hunter held his spear against the hook, with the shaft lying along the rod of the thrower. Then he raised the whole thing above his shoulder and, with a powerful overhand motion, let the spear go. The length of the spear thrower, added to that of the hunter's arm, gave more force to the cast, and the hook pushed the spear forward much farther than would otherwise have been possible. A spear thus became a more deadly weapon. Spear throwers were cherished possessions, and many of those that have been found are beautifully decorated with carved figures of animals.

For fishing, the hunters made harpoons, and fish gorges — short pieces of wood or bone with a line tied midway between their two pointed ends. When bait was wrapped around one of these gorges and a fish swallowed it, the line tightened and the gorge stuck crosswise in the fish's throat, hooking him securely.

Out of bone, ivory, and antler the hunters shaped other useful objects — hammers, awls, chisels, wedges, buttons, needles. The needles were probably used in sewing skins to make clothing. Human beings would have needed some protection against the cold weather.

Of course, they had fire, too. The many hearths in the caves show that. And in among the charcoal, lying close together, are flint and iron pyrites, a mineral. These two are a fire-making combination: when struck together, they will make a spark. Evidently the hunters had learned how to start a blaze whenever they needed one — a valuable skill.

Evidently, too, they knew about cooking their meat. The animal bones among the clutter on the cave floors have been heated by fire.

A hunter's necklace.

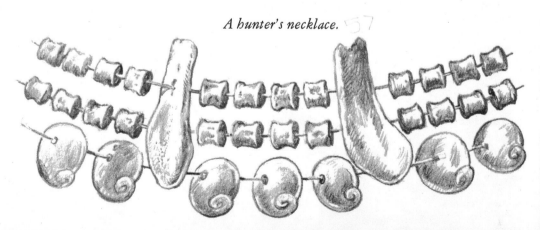

A hunter in his finery.

All in all, as living went in those days, the valley hunters must have had a fairly easy time of it. Indeed, they lived well enough so that they could spend some of their time on what might be called luxuries. They appear to have carried on trade with people on the coast of the Mediterranean. Seashells from that shore, and the bones of sea fish, turn up in the inland caves.

And the hunters seem to have spent time and thought in making decorations to wear. Skeletons of their dead are found, carefully buried in graves. In death, they wear the finery that must have been theirs in life. There are fancy caps made of pierced shells and animals' teeth, strung together. And there are ornamental belts, bracelets, elbow bangles, knee bands, and decorated loincloths. In addition to shells, teeth, and the usual ivory, animal bone, and antler, the most common materials used in making the hunters' finery were bird bones, backbones of fish, and bright stones.

47

But the hunters' artistic skill went far beyond carving decorations on their spear throwers and other possessions, and making necklaces and headdresses. The most astonishing thing about these people is their so-called "cave art," the pictures that they made on the walls of their caves and shelters.

The story of the discovery of this art is interesting. From time to time in the past century, explorers had noticed, on cave walls, scratches and lines that looked like drawings, but had given little thought to them. Then one day in 1878 a little Spanish girl visited a cave on the hill of Altamira, in Spain, where her father, Don Marcelino De Sautuola, was digging for flints and other remains of prehistoric men.

This digging was a slow, painstaking business, and after a while the girl became bored with it. As she wandered about the cave, she tilted her light upward, and gasped in surprise. Pictured on the rock above her, there suddenly appeared a colorful multitude of huge animals.

"*Toros*," she called to her father, "*toros*!" *Toros* is the Spanish word for "bulls," and it was thus that these animals appeared to her.

Her father, thinking that the shadows in the cave had deceived her eyes, nevertheless put down his tools and came to look. Now it was his turn to gasp. There above him, magnificently painted in red, yellow, and black, was a host of enormous bison, an animal species that had disappeared from Spain in prehistoric times. In the dim, flickering light, the beasts were so lifelike that they almost seemed to be stamping across the roof of the cave.

De Sautuola was impressed, yet puzzled, and he and his daughter began to look further. More and more drawings came to light, and gradually De Sautuola realized that here, on the walls and ceiling, was a great and important find.

Up to this time, people had thought of the cave dwellers as unfeeling savages whose lives were spent in one long search for food. But, preserved in the damp and dark of this cave, were wonderful pictures that remained exactly as they had been painted thousands and thousands of years before, by these very same cavemen. De Sautuola was convinced of that.

A bison on the cave ceiling, Altamira, Spain.

As he searched, he found lumps of ocher, the iron oxide that furnished the red and yellow colors of the paintings, and charcoal, which furnished the black. He found stones on which the colors had been ground into powder, to be mixed with grease, then applied to the cave surfaces. And, further to prove that the drawings were the work of the ancient cave dwellers, he found places where water, dissolving minerals from the rocks, had run down and deposited over the pictures a transparent mineral glaze that must have taken thousands of years to form.

And what pictures these were! There was nothing of the beginner about them. They were the work of experienced artists who had keen eyes for everything about the creatures they were drawing — who had a good idea of the pictures they wanted to paint — and who were able to carry out their ideas into finished work.

And these men were not only artists; they were hunters, as well. They knew how a bison looked in life — fleeing, angry, wounded, at bay, or standing quietly. Here, on the rocks, they had pictured the animals with breathtaking skill.

Painting them could not have been easy. The cave was pitch-dark, and as light, the artists must have had to use torches or bowl-like stone lamps, burning some sort of grease as fuel, and moss as a wick. Many of the pictures were high on the walls and on the ceiling. In order to reach them, the artists must have had to climb up the walls or stand on the shoulders of their comrades. Or possibly they used rough wooden ladders.

The walls and ceiling of the cave were rough, and there were many swellings and hollows in the rock. But the artists had made

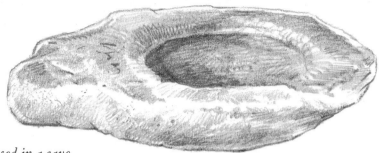

Stone lamp, used in a cave.

these roughnesses work for them. A picture might be placed so that a bump in the stone became a bison's shoulder or rump; a hollow might be made to show the modeling of the animal's body. And the artists had added their colors in such a way that the beasts did not seem to lie flat, but to stand forth, living and in the round.

Although De Sautuola was tremendously interested in prehistoric men, he was not an expert on them. He realized the importance of the discovery he had made, however, and he hurried to call in a friend who was a geologist, to explore his cave. This man was also impressed, and De Sautuola prepared a report of his find, which he published in 1880.

But here he met a setback. None of the experts believed him. "Impossible!" they said. "The cave dwellers were dolts and savages. They could not have created this magnificent art. There must be some fraud."

De Sautuola had taken an artist friend into the cave, to copy some of the paintings as illustrations for his report. When the experts learned this, they were certain that they knew just what the fraud was, and who had painted the cave pictures. Try as he might, De Sautuola could not convince them that these paintings had truly been made centuries before. The fight about them raged for years.

In spite of the doubts of the experts, however, De Sautuola's report had started them thinking. They began to take their eyes off their diggings on the cave floors long enough to look at the walls. And they began to find paintings in other caves and to see for themselves that these pictures could not have been made in recent times. Slowly most of them were won over to De Sautuola's side. It was not until after his death, however, that the last of the experts admitted his mistake in not believing De Sautuola.

Today it is recognized that the Magdalenians created the art in their caves. And further, it is recognized that they were not the first to do this. Long before their day, their ancestors, the Aurignacians, were painting the lively little wild horses that caper through the cave at Lascaux, in France, and were drawing other masterly pictures there and elsewhere. The ancient cave art is found throughout northern Spain and southwestern France.

Wild horses pictured in the cave, Lascaux, France.

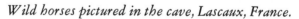

Stencils of hands, and wavy lines on a cave wall. These stencils were made by placing hands on the rock and applying color around them.

Judging by the earliest known examples, this art seems to have begun with wavy lines which the cave dwellers traced with their fingers in the damp clay of some cave walls, and with stencils of their hands which they made by placing their palms in coloring matter, then slapping them flat on the rock. The hunters also made simple outlines of animals. Gradually, as the centuries went by, artists began to draw more details. They filled in their outlines with color, which they put on with a pad or brush, or perhaps sometimes sprayed on by blowing it through some sort of tube. Finally they were able to create the beautiful red, yellow, and black creatures of Altamira and other caves, shaded in color so that they appeared to be living animals in three dimensions.

We cannot help but wonder why the hunters painted these pictures. Except in a few cases, it certainly was not for decoration. Nor could it have been for pleasure. Most of the paintings were not made in the caves where the hunters lived. And many of them are deep within the earth, in the caverns' darkest and most distant corners, often where they can be arrived at only by crawling through narrow passageways or over slippery clay and sharp pebbles. Many are made on parts of the walls that could only have been reached with great difficulty. And often a painting has been made directly on top of an older one, without regard for looks or the ruining of the earlier picture.

Besides the paintings, there are animals modeled in clay, sculptured in relief, or engraved in the solid rock wall with a burin. But wherever the pictures are in northern Spain or southwestern France, and whatever the method used in making them, all the art does have some things in common.

Sometimes, to reach his work, an artist may have stood on a comrade's shoulders.

This stone-carved animal is adapted to the natural shape of the rock.

The colored paintings all make use of oxide of iron for red and yellow, and oxide of manganese, or sometimes charcoal, for black or brown. The coloring has all been put on the rock by the same means — pads, brushes, or blowers. And almost all the paintings are of the animals that the hunters must have thought of most often. There are bison, mammoths, reindeer, woolly rhinoceroses, wild horses, wild cattle — all excellent food. There are a few cave bears and lions — both enemies whom the hunters wanted to kill.

The artists have taken great pains to make the animals as lifelike as possible, but the very few pictures of men are poorly done. There are almost no drawings of plants, and there is no background scenery.

Everything seems to show that most of the pictures were made for some practical purpose. Probably the hunters had some idea of magic: they may have thought that by painting an animal deep in a cave they could gain some power over the living creature. In this way they could make sure that its numbers would increase and that it would be easy to kill.

Some of the art may picture the hunters' hopes. By painting a beast wounded by a spear, as is sometimes the case, the artist may have been trying to make a wish come true.

Some of the pictures may have played a part in ceremonies to ensure good hunting. On the clay floor in front of some of them are the ancient footprints of many hunters.

No one can be sure of all the reasons for the cave paintings. But whatever their purpose, they hold their place with the great art of all the ages.

They could not ensure a steady supply of game animals, however, and when the glaciers melted northward for the last time, the cold-weather animals of the tundra either followed the ice or died out. The great herds with their generous food supply were gone, and the cave dwellers no longer had an easy living with leisure for their art. It came to an end.

Ceremonies may have been performed in the caves to ensure good hunting.

After the Glaciers

WITH THE FINAL shrinking of the glaciers (about 10,000 B.C.), Europe became a very different place from what it had been in the days of the mammoth hunters and the Magdalenians. The water from the melted ice gradually drained into the sea, and forest trees slowly spread over what had been open tundra covered with grasses and shrubs. The climate grew warmer, and elk, red deer, beavers, wild pigs, hares, and brown bears — dwellers of the forest — became the common animals of the time.

New ways of living were needed to meet the new conditions, and here men showed what an advantage they had over the animals. In this warmer land, the mammoths and some of the other creatures had died out because their bodies could not change quickly enough to fit them to their new surroundings. But the bodies of human beings did not need to change. Humans had only to wear lighter clothing, to find new food, and to make some changes in their tools and weapons. Here their brains served them well. The people of those times were able to invent the necessary new ways of doing things.

No longer barred by the glaciers, groups of men and women, with their children, roamed throughout Europe and parts of Asia, as well as Africa, living in a variety of places — in the forest, on the shores of lakes or the sea, along riverbanks. Each group worked out methods of getting the best food and shelter it could from its surroundings. Even more than in Paleolithic days, there were many ways of living in this time after the glaciers that is called the *Meso-*

lithic, or *Middle Stone*, *Age*. Before the Mesolithic Age was over (some time after 6000 B.C.), man had spread over much of the earth.

Among the varying ways of living in the Mesolithic Age, some things stand out.

The spear was no longer the favorite weapon. Almost all the forest hunters used the bow and arrow, instead. Here was the best weapon invented by man up to this time.

In pulling back an arrow before shooting, the hunter slowly stored in it all the energy of his arm and shoulder muscles. When he let the arrow go, this stored-up energy was suddenly freed all at one time, to drive the arrow toward its target with a much more

The Mesolithic hunters had bows and arrows and dogs to help them.

deadly force than that of a spear. Besides that, the hunter could shoot an arrow from a greater distance than he could throw a spear. It flew silently. If he missed his first shot he could fit another arrow to his bow and try again, still from a distance, before his prey even suspected he was there.

The bow and arrow shows the advantage of man over the animals once again. No creature but man with his large brain could have thought of it. And no creature but man could possibly have shot it. His upright position freed his hands; his grasping fingers held the bow firm and pulled back the arrow; and his distance-judging eyes made possible his accurate aim.

Besides bows and arrows, the Mesolithic people had another help in hunting: namely, dogs. Their bones, slightly different from those of wild animals of the same family, have been found in the remains of Mesolithic dwelling places. From savage, wolfish creatures that lurked around the camps, stealing whatever bones and scraps of meat they could snatch, dogs somehow became men's partners in the search for game. With their sharp hearing and keen noses for scent, they were better able than men to track down the beasts of the forest. For their help they were rewarded with a share of the kill. Men were learning that animals might be valuable for something besides food and raw materials. If tamed, they could be employed in useful work.

But even with the help of bows and arrows and dogs, the hunters must have found that the forest animals did not furnish enough meat. People were forced to fall back on other kinds of food.

The women must have gathered many kinds of plants; charred

hazelnuts and wild pears have been found in the ashes of the camp-fires. In addition, wild birds and fish became important foods. The Mesolithic people made barbed fish harpoons and used barbless fish-hooks. Fishing traps and fishing nets with floats and sinkers have been found, preserved in the silt of the Baltic Sea. And along the north European seacoasts are great piles of bones and shells, cast there by Mesolithic groups who lived largely on sea fish and shell-fish.

Now that trees covered Europe, there was a good supply of wood. The forest people made themselves the necessary tools for working

Fishermen on the coast made fishing traps and nets.

Some of the northern people made sledges.

with it: axes, wedges, adzes, and other such implements of stone and bone. Many wooden objects dating from Mesolithic times have been found, preserved in the bogs of Finland and Sweden. Among them are large paddle rudders that must have been used in some kind of boat, probably a dugout canoe. In Finland, skis and the runners of sledges have also been found, showing that some of these people had land transportation over snow and ice.

For dwelling places, some of the Mesolithic people seem to have had huts and tents. Many of the hunters, in chasing game, must have kept moving over a large territory. In that case, they probably still made use of caves, rock overhangs, and shelters dug out of the earth.

By making whatever changes were necessary in the Paleolithic ways of doing things, the Mesolithic people were able to live. But, like the Paleolithic people before them, they were hunters and gatherers, with no real control over their food supply. As long as the hunting and fishing and gathering were good, the Mesolithic people could survive. But they had no means of making sure that their animal and plant supply would last. Some more certain way of getting food was needed.

The First Farmers

WHILE THE Mesolithic people in Europe carried on the old ways of hunting and gathering, something exciting was happening in what is now the Near East, at the eastern end of the Mediterranean. Some time between the years 8000 and 5000 B.C., people in this area took one of the most important steps in the whole history of man, from the very beginning to the present day. *They learned to domesticate plants and animals.* That is, they began to raise their own crops of vegetable foods instead of merely gathering wild plants; and they found certain animals that would depend on man for food and protection without running away — animals, moreover, that would have their young in captivity, so ensuring new flocks.

In short, these people discovered farming.

What's so exciting about that? you may be saying. But think! When they learned to domesticate plants and animals, they freed themselves, and men forever after, from their complete dependence on hunting and gathering — both of them rather chancy ways of getting food. From then on, they were able to plan and control part of their own food supply, except in extraordinary times when drought or some other disaster interfered.

This period when man first became a farmer is called the *Neolithic*, or *New Stone*, *Age*, because of its new methods of making stone tools. Now, instead of pressing flakes from a stone to pro-

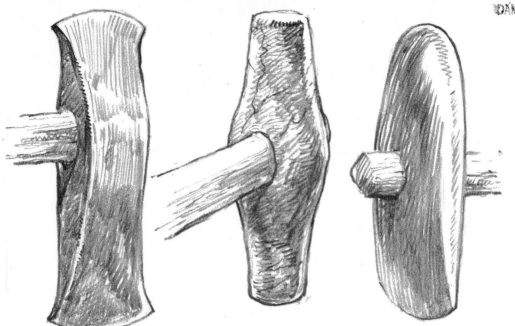

Tools of polished stone.

duce a sharp edge, men changed to grinding it by rubbing it against a rough material such as sandstone, emery, or sand, as they had sometimes finished bone and antler in earlier times. This sort of rubbing made a smooth, highly polished stone tool with many advantages. But, in spite of the name Neolithic (New Stone), the most important thing about this age still remains man's solving the problem of his food supply.

Nowadays everyone takes farming for granted. But for the Neolithic people, whose ancestors for thousands of years had depended on wild plants and animals, farming was a difficult step, and it took imagination. In fact, the domestication of plants and animals must have happened very slowly. Long before any crops were raised by farmers, the women who collected wild food may have had favorite

63

spots where plants grew particularly well and where their seeds or fruits were especially large. The women may have protected these places for themselves, driving away wild birds and animals who foraged there.

Perhaps the women may also have noticed that seeds which were accidentally dropped around a campsite grew especially well in soil which was enriched by the refuse of the camp. And they may have protected these plants, too, until they produced a crop. Gradually the idea of purposely sowing the seeds of particularly good plants may then have developed.

No one is sure just when or how the first steps in crop-raising were taken, but archeologists have unearthed villages dating back probably earlier than 6000 B.C., in which farming seems already to have been the established way of life.

Man's first successfully domesticated plants were wheat and barley. These two grains grew wild in the Near East. Domesticated, their seeds became much larger, and were naturally a good crop for farmers. They were high in food value; they were easy to store; they lasted well and were still good after several years; they were simple to plant and harvest, and needed little care while they were growing; their stalks were good fodder for animals and could be used for other things as well, such as thatching the roofs of houses.

People had already used wild wheat and barley, and so they had the tools for dealing with these plants. At first, they probably cultivated their fields with pointed digging sticks like the ones the gatherers had used for collecting edible roots. For cutting the ripe grain, they used sickles made by setting small flint blades into slots in a straight piece of bone or wood. After the seeds had been separated from the plants by threshing, the women ground them to flour in hand mills similar to those stones on which the Paleolithic artists had mashed their colors into powder.

After the crops had been harvested, the farmers probably turned their animals into the fields, to graze on the plant stalks. The earliest successfully domesticated animals, besides the dog, were ones that we still find valuable today: goats, pigs, sheep, and cattle. As with the plants, no one is sure just how these animals were first domesticated. Perhaps it all began when a few of the young were kept more or less as pets. When they grew older, they may still have hung about the settlements. If, in time, they had young ones, these

Stone tools of the early farmers: hoe of the later Neolithic, with polished stone head restored (left); later Neolithic flint sickle blade (right); in upper center is a stone hand mill for grinding grain; below it, an early antler sickle, with flint teeth restored.

animals may have been even tamer. Gradually, then, the idea may have grown of purposely keeping the tamest animals in flocks, for the milk and meat and hides they produced and for the work they might do.

Man never could have started raising plants and animals if he had not been able to plan ahead and to put aside some of what he had gained, for use in the future.

In the case of plants, he was willing to work in his fields all season without any reward until harvesttime. And even then he did not eat all his grain quickly, but stored some of it to feed himself and his family until the next harvest was ripe — usually a year later. More than that, he was willing to return some of the grain to the soil, as seed, at the next planting.

In the case of animals, he learned not to kill them at once for food, as men had in Paleolithic times. Instead, he kept the best milkgivers and wool bearers for the things they could furnish him besides meat. And he spared the tamest and strongest animals so that they could produce young and increase his flocks.

At the same time, men did not give up hunting, fishing, and gathering. They simply added the new habits of farming to the older ways of living. But, in time, by their own work in the fields they were able to produce a good deal of what they ate. Whatever they got from hunting, fishing, and gathering was simply that much extra, and the old ways of obtaining food became less and less important.

Farming brought many changes in men's ways of living.

The Mesolithic hunting people needed to roam over a wide area in order to find their food. They had to be continually on the move, and often they did not have permanent dwellings, but lived in a series of camps. Too many hunters spoiled the hunting; they therefore lived in very small groups.

When the farmers sowed a crop, however, they had to stay in one place to tend and protect it and to harvest it when it was ripe. There was an advantage in living near other people, moreover, so that the whole group could help with some tasks. The farmers therefore lived in villages which lasted over a period of years.

The farmers' food supply was larger and more regular than that of the Mesolithic hunters. And even quite small children could help in the fields. It was an advantage to farmers to support larger families than hunters ever could. If, after a number of years, the land around a village became worn out from being constantly planted, some of the people — or all of them — could move to a new spot, clear more land, and start a new settlement. After farming began, the world became much more thickly populated.

Living in villages meant living in permanent houses, and in Neolithic times more thought began to be put into building these dwelling places. They often differed somewhat from village to village and were made of a variety of materials: reeds and dried mud, dried mud alone, woven branches plastered with clay, or logs, or stone. They were rectangular in shape and had one or more rooms. Their roofs were often thatched with reeds or straw, or made of branches bound together.

Now that grain was an important food, the women must have given new thought to ways of cooking it. One of the easiest meth-

ods is boiling. Water placed in a pit lined with hides can be made to boil by dropping hot stones into it. But boiling is best done in a pot that will hold water and can be placed over a fire. In Mesolithic times, woven reed baskets had been used for gathering plant foods. These baskets, daubed with a coating of clay, might serve the purpose of boiling-pots, and perhaps they did in early Neolithic times. In any case, the Neolithic people somehow discovered that clay,

A Neolithic farming village of the Near East.

when heated to a high point, turned into an altogether different material, which was fireproof, waterproof, and hard enough to hold its shape and not break unless it received a hard blow. They invented pottery.

Now that they had settled in one place and their food supply was certain, they had time to spend on things other than finding their next meal. Making a pot was a somewhat complicated business, but they were able to work it out. First, the proper clay must be found. It could not be used just as it was, however; a small amount of straw or sand — a "temper" — must be added in order that the pot would hold its shape and harden without cracking. Next, the pot must be formed. The Neolithic people made their pots by rolling clay into coils, then placing one coil above another and molding them all together. After this, the pot must be placed in the sun until some of its moisture dried out. Finally, when it was baked in a very hot fire, more moisture left the clay and it became pottery.

At first, pottery in the Near East was crude and undecorated, but later, as the Bronze Age neared, it was painted with various designs, some quite elaborate.

Through pottery the Neolithic people made an important discovery: by treating one kind of material — in this case, a lump of clay — in a special way, they could make an entirely different material of it. And, with pottery, they were no longer limited by the shape and size of their raw material, as they had been with stone, antler, and bone. Potters could make containers as large as they wished, in whatever form they might fancy.

Besides creating pottery from clay, the Neolithic people invented another process for changing one material into another. They wove linen cloth from the flax plant, and later made fabric from sheep's wool.

It was perhaps even more difficult to figure out how to make linen cloth than how to make pottery. First, the necessary fibers had to be separated from the stalks of flax. Next, these short fibers had to be spun together into one continuous thread. And finally, the thread had somehow to be woven into cloth.

The Neolithic people were ingenious enough to solve all the problems of clothmaking. In the ruins of their villages are round, pierced stones called "spindle whorls," used to weight a spindle and make it whirl, so twisting into thread the fibers that the women attached to it. For weaving, they invented looms with bars at the top and bottom to form a frame, to which vertical threads were attached. As other threads were woven over and under these, the women used a comb to push them tightly together, thus making a firm fabric. And they thought of many other helpful devices. Even today, our power-driven looms are based on the weaving inventions of the Neolithic people.

Pierced stone whorls were used to weight spindles and make them whirl as thread was spun.

In Neolithic times the women did the weaving and potmaking, as well as the cultivating of domesticated plants, the collecting of wild ones, the cooking of food, and the supervising of the youngest children. The men cleared the plots of ground for farming, tended the farm animals, hunted and fished, did the carpentry work, and made their own tools and weapons. All but the very young children must have helped with the crops and herds and gathered wild plants for food.

Besides dividing the work in this way, the villagers must also have had some simple rules for getting along together: to regulate such things as what land was to be planted by each person and what reserved for grazing animals — and other problems that might arise from living close together in a farming community.

As time went on, various kinds of crude looms were used for weaving cloth.
On this loom, the vertical threads are weighted, to hold them taut.

Because each separate village was self-supporting and had its own way of doing things, probably no two settlements were alike. There was a good deal of trading from village to village of such things as flint, amber, seashells, and semiprecious stones, however, and there is no doubt that men had long since mastered language fully. Through visiting back and forth, the people of the various villages must have exchanged ideas and shared any invention or discovery they might have made.

A Firm Foundation

NOT ALL the ancient people took to Neolithic ways of living at one and the same time. Farming started in the Near East, but slowly the farmers and their ways spread out along the northern coast of Africa and over into Europe, and also up the Danube River valley and on into the north. In many areas the Mesolithic hunters continued to live for a long time not far from the Neolithic farmers. By 1000 B.C., however, farming had become the established way of life throughout Europe, the Near East, North Africa, and many other parts of the world.

Long before 1000 B.C., however, the people of the Near East had made another discovery: how to use copper and bronze. For these people, the Stone Age had ended by 3000 B.C., and the Bronze Age — when metal was first used — had begun. This age brought with it many exciting inventions and discoveries.

The new ways of the Bronze Age, however, arose from the solid foundations laid by the Stone Age people. These ancient folk had started their career over a million years earlier, as primitive and

By 1000 B.C., *farming was an established way of life, and some farmers were using a plow; for many people the Stone Age was over and the Bronze Age had begun.*

ignorant inhabitants of the world. Little by little, slowly and painfully, they had learned to live in their surroundings. By adopting new ways as the world around them changed, human beings had survived when many of the animals had died out. At first, men had been rare creatures, but their numbers had increased until, by Mesolithic times, they were rapidly spreading over the earth.

They had lived in the open and in a variety of dwelling places — caves, rock shelters, tents, pit huts — until finally they had learned to build houses.

During most of the Stone Age they had depended on hunting wild animals and gathering wild plants as food, but at last, toward the very end of the period, they had become farmers — producers of a regular food supply.

Eating their food raw at first, they had mastered fire, then cooking, and finally had invented a practical cooking utensil — pottery.

Wearing no clothes in the beginning, they had used, as their first covering, the rough skins of animals; later they had sewed the skins into garments; and in Neolithic times they had invented the weaving of fabrics.

Beginning with rough choppers and hand axes, they had become ever more skilled in making tools, until they were producing bows and arrows, polished stone axes, and beautifully decorated implements of ivory, bone, and antler.

Probably starting with little ability to talk, or to think about much but the hard problems of keeping alive, they had mastered spoken language and had become artists, inventors, and traders.

76

The Stone Age people were the original pioneers. They were the first to face human problems. More than anyone since, they had to invent and experiment. By the end of the Stone Age they had shaped a way of living that served not only as a foundation for the Bronze Age folk to build on, but for the people of the world ever since. We owe them our thanks.

Other Books to Read

BAUMANN, HANS   *The Caves of the Great Hunters*   Pantheon
  1954

FRIEDMAN, ESTELLE   *Man in the Making*   Putnam   1960

QUENNELL, MARJORIE   *Everyday Life in Prehistoric Times*
  Putnam   1959

WHITE, ANNE TERRY   *The First Men in the World*   Harper
  1958

Index

FIRST BOOKS
classified by subject
Some titles are listed in more than one category

The ARTS

Architecture
Ballet
Bells
Color
Drawing

Gardening
How to Fix It
Jazz
Music
Paintings
Photography

Poetry
Puppets
Rhythms
Stage Costume and
   Make-Up

COMMUNICATIONS

Atlas
Codes and Ciphers
Language & How To
   Use It

Letter Writing
Maps and Globes
Measurement
Printing

Public Libraries
Teaching Machines
Television
Words

SCIENCE

Air
Airplanes
Antarctic
Archaeology
Architecture
Astronomy
Automobiles
Bees
Bells
Birds
Bridges
Bugs
Caves
Color
Conservation
Cotton
Earth

Electricity
Food
Glaciers
Glass
Human Senses
Light
Machines
Mammals
Maps and Globes
Measurement
Microbes
Mining
Ocean
Photography
Plants
Prehistoric Animals
Rhythms

Roads
Science Experiments
Sea Shells
Snakes
Sound
Space Travel
Stone Age Man
Stones
Submarines
Television
Tools
Trains
Trees
Tropical Mammals
Water
Weather
Wild Flowers

SPORTS & HOBBIES

Baseball
Basketball
Boys' Cooking
Cartoons for Kids
Cats
Chess
Christmas Joy
Codes and Ciphers

Dogs
Dolls
Football
Gardening
Horses
How to Fix It
Jokes
Magic

Photography
Physical Fitness
Sailing
Stones
Surprising Facts
Swimming

SOCIAL STUDIES
United States

Atlas
American History
American Revolution
California Gold Rush
The China Clippers
Civil War Land Battles
Civil War Naval Actions
Congress
Constitution
Early Settlers

Hawaii
Holidays
Indian Wars
Indians
National Monuments
National Parks
Negroes
New England
New World Explorers

Oregon Trail
Panama Canal
Pioneers
Presidents
Supreme Court
United Nations
War of 1812
Washington, D.C.
World War I
World War II

The World About Us

Africa
Ancient Bible Lands
Ancient Egypt
Ancient Mesopotamia
   and Persia
Ancient Greece
Ancient Rome
Antarctic
Archaeology
Australia
Barbarian Invaders
Brazil
Canada

Communist China
Congo
England
Eskimos
Festivals
France
Ghana
India
Israel
Italy
Japan
Kings
Medieval Man
Mediterranean

Mexico
Netherlands
New Zealand
Ocean
Pakistan
South America
Soviet Union
United Nations
Vikings
West Germany
West Indies
World War I
World War II

People and Products

Conservation
Cotton
Cowboys

Firemen
Food
Glass

Nurses
Supermarkets
Water

LITERATURE & LANGUAGE ARTS

Codes and Ciphers
Color
Fairy Tales
Language & How To
   Use It

Letter Writing
Legendary Beings
Maps and Globes
Mythology
Mythical Beasts

Norse Legends
Poetry
Printing
Teaching Machines
Words

TRANSPORTATION

Airplanes
Automobiles
Boats
Bridges

Maps and Globes
Panama Canal
Roads
Ships

Space Travel
Trains
Water